HOW TO INTERPRET THE PSYCHOLOGY OF RESOLUTIONS FOR THE NEW YEAR.

BY

Dr TIMOTHY KESSINGTON.

approval from the publisher or creator.

TABLE OF CONTENTS

ABOUT THE AUTHOR

INTRODUCTION.

TABLE OF CONTENT

HOW TO INTERPRET THE PSYCHOLOGY OF RESOLUTIONS FOR THE NEW YEAR.

INTRODUCTION

CHAPTER 1. Determine your main relationship objectives.

CHAPTER 2. Communicate your objectives to your spouse.

CHAPTER 3. Create an action plan.

CHAPTER 4. Include relationship-building practices.

CHAPTER 5. Seek assistance when required.

CHAPTER 6. Adopt an adaptable mindset.

CHAPTER 7. Put self-care first.

CONCLUSION.

ABOUT THE AUTHOR

Dr. TIMOTHY KESSINGTON is a licensed psychologist in the state of texas. he is a certified counselor on marriage and relationship/mental health. He is passionate to the core to see people in relationships happy and couples achieve the best out of every relationship.

INTRODUCTION

Examining the psychology of New Year's resolutions might provide light on how to stay committed to your relationship objectives.

Comprehending the fundamental elements that determine whether a resolve succeeds or fails may enable people to overcome obstacles, cultivating a more robust bond and enduring dedication in their partnerships all through the year.

Knowing the psychology behind our resolution-making

Examining the psychology of New Year's resolutions offers important insights into people's propensity to make life-changing objectives.

Examining the driving forces, mental processes, and cultural influences behind these commitments may provide light on methods for developing goals that are meaningful and strengthening the resolve required to accomplish personal development in the next year.

Effect of a Fresh Start. The appeal of New Year's goals is increased by the fascinating psychological phenomenon known as the "Fresh Start Effect." This cognitive bias, which has its roots in the psychology of New Year's resolutions, encourages hope and drive, inspiring people to work towards life-changing objectives. Gaining knowledge about this phenomenon increases the possibility that a resolution will be successful by enabling ways to harness its power.

The significance of goal-setting
The psychology of New Year's resolutions heavily relies on goal setting. People may use this knowledge to set specific,

attainable goals by knowing the subtleties in the psychology of New Year's resolutions. They can overcome obstacles and accomplish long-lasting success in their goals because this engages motivational factors that promote dedication and perseverance.

The development of habits and resistance to change
The development of habits and reluctance to change are closely linked to the psychology of New Year's resolutions. People may overcome the difficulty of

adopting new habits by having a better understanding of the psychological dynamics. It is possible to successfully integrate beneficial behavioubehaviorsrease the chance of continuous commitment to goals throughout the year by identifying and overcoming opposition. Overcoming obstacles and staying inspired RecognisiRecognizingcoming obstacles in the psychology of New Year's resolutions calls for fortitude. By accepting the subtle psychological aspects of making resolutions, people may stay motivated when confronted with obstacles. Acknowledging obstacles as chances for improvement and adapting tactics encourages persistent dedication, guaranteeing ongoing advancement toward a successful resolution.

Which relationship-related New Year's goals are most popular? Relationship goals are a common way for people to start a new year and demonstrate their dedication to both personal and interpersonal development. This is understood as the "new year, new me"

mentality. Typical goals include:
Encouraging better dialogue
Setting aside time for quality
Improving closeness and
emotional connection
establishing shared objectives
Gaining expertise in resolving
conflicts
Taking care of oneself
fostering a common interest
Increasing Confidence
Gratitude
Together, these goals show a
commitment to positive change
and a fresh emphasis on creating a
more happy and successful
relationship in the future year.

CHAPTER 1. Determine your main relationship objectives.

By embracing the psychology of New Year's resolutions, determining your primary relationship objectives turns into a meaningful exercise in dedication and introspection. Examining what counts, think about the goals that fit with the fresh start that the new year represents.

Grounding your relationship objectives in the psychology of resolutions today offers the groundwork for meaningful connection and constructive development, whatever of the goals—better communication, more intimacy, or mutual progress. Couples that go through this self-examination process are better equipped to start the new year with intention and build a strong, happy bond.

CHAPTER 2. Communicate your objectives to your spouse.

Examining the psychology of New Year's resolutions, talking to your spouse about your relationship objectives may have a transforming effect. A common vision is created via sharing ambitions, which strengthens bonds of dedication and solidarity. This psychological alignment increases motivation by making use of the momentum created by the new year and the fresh start impact.

Being honest about personal preferences and expectations fosters understanding and strengthens the basis for group goal-setting. Couples strengthen their bond and lay the groundwork for a year of mutual development by incorporating the psychology of resolutions into this conversation, which highlights the importance of their relationship goals in the next months.

CHAPTER 3. Create an action plan.

In the context of the psychology around New Year's resolutions, creating a game plan for your relationship objectives is a calculated and proactive move. During this process, broad goals are broken down into manageable stages, making use of the drive that comes with a fresh start. Setting attainable goals helps people overcome the cognitive biases connected to new beginnings, which strengthens commitment and endurance.

The act of planning itself supports
a feeling of purpose and control
and is consistent with the
psychological concepts that guide
the effective execution of
resolutions. Your relationship
objectives will become concrete
and attainable over the year with
this deliberate method.

CHAPTER 4. Include relationship-building practices.

Relationship-building practices fit very well with the psychology of New Year's resolutions. The cultivation of constructive behaviors that advance the partnership's well-being is a key component of this deliberate integration. By acknowledging the transformational potential of habits within the context of resolutions, couples can use the drive that comes with fresh starts.

This psychological alignment facilitates the development of behaviors that enhance mutual assistance, connection, and communication. By representing the spirit of positive change and progress that is inherent in the psychology of resolutions connected with the new year, these habits, as they become established, contribute to the ongoing accomplishment of relationship objectives throughout the year.

CHAPTER 5. Seek assistance when required.

Understanding the psychology of New Year's resolutions and asking for help in relationships when necessary becomes essential to achieving your goals. This acknowledgment accepts the innate human desire for support and encouragement.
Seeking help is consistent with the shared responsibility concept, whether it is done via clear and honest conversation with your spouse, confiding in reliable

friends, or seeking professional advice.

It makes use of the new beginning effect to promote motivation and resilience. This psychological support not only fortifies the individual's dedication but also fosters the group's efforts to achieve relationship objectives. When it comes to resolutions, asking for help turns into a proactive move toward conquering obstacles and creating enduring relationships.

CHAPTER 6. Adopt an adaptable mindset.

In the context of relationship objectives, embracing flexibility is consistent with the psychology of New Year's resolutions. Understanding that goals, objectives, and personal requirements might change, success depends on one's ability to be flexible. Couples may overcome unforeseen obstacles and reevaluate their objectives as needed because of this psychological flexibility.

Partners maintain commitment and cultivate resilience via accepting change. Since flexibility and the new start effect are inherently linked, the relationship will always be dynamic and sensitive to how life changes. This psychological strategy fosters understanding between the parties and supports the relationship's yearly development and flexibility.

CHAPTER 7. Put self-care first.

Following the psychology of New Year's resolutions, it is important to prioritize self-care to achieve relationship objectives. This deliberate attention acknowledges the importance of each person's well-being to the success of a relationship.

Couples strengthen their emotional resilience and cultivate a positive outlook that enhances the relationship by using self-care routines.

In keeping with the psychology of the new year, putting self-care first serves as a basis for personal development and fosters a more harmonious and satisfying relationship. This dedication to personal well-being strengthens the alliance and creates a nurturing atmosphere that makes it easier to accomplish common objectives all year long.

How can I make my relationship objectives attainable and realistic? Determine the expectations and wants of both partners to establish reasonable and attainable relationship goals. Set clear goals, give priority to good communication, and take into account each other's advantages and disadvantages.

To maintain continuous development and achievement in the relationship, break down big objectives into smaller, more achievable milestones that you can review and tweak as necessary.

What are some typical mistakes people make while trying to resolve their relationships?

When attempting to mend a relationship, common mistakes include having high expectations, not communicating well, and ignoring personal needs. Steer clear of making comparisons to other relationships, assigning blame instead of working together to resolve problems, and pushing for change without considering your partner's point of view. The effectiveness of a settlement depends on fostering flexibility and mutual understanding.

How can I stay motivated and dedicated to my relationship objectives all year long?

To stay motivated and committed to your relationship objectives, review and congratulate your accomplishments regularly. Make open communication a priority and work as a team to overcome obstacles. Establish reasonable expectations and foster shared experiences. Goals should be frequently reevaluated and adjusted to reflect changing conditions.

Encourage one another's personal development to build a strong and lasting relationship.

How do I respond to arguments or disputes that come up when we work towards our relationship's objectives?

When pursuing relationship goals, approach disagreements with empathy and attentive listening. Strive for compromise, communicate honestly, and express your emotions without placing blame. When feelings are too strong, take a break and come back to the talk composed. Work together to address problems and concentrate on common goals to strengthen your connection even in the face of conflict.

CONCLUSION.

To maintain relationship objectives in the new year, one must comprehend the psychology behind resolutions. Make good communication a priority, acknowledge achievements, and be flexible when faced with obstacles.

To achieve long-term success, think about enlarging your relationship adventure in the next year and beyond, encouraging development, and getting expert advice like counseling or classes.